Sports Illustrated KIDS

THE PATHS TO PRO

BASKETBALL

by Matt Doeden

Capstone Captivate is published by Capstone Press, an imprint of Capstone.
1710 Roe Crest Drive
North Mankato, Minnesota 56003
www.capstonepub.com
SPORTS ILLUSTRATED KIDS is a trademark of ABG-SI LLC. Used with permission.

Library of Congress Cataloging-in-Publication Data
Names: Doeden, Matt, author.
Title: The paths to pro basketball / by Matt Doeden.
Description: North Mankato, Minnesota : Capstone Captivate is published by Capstone Press, [2021] | Series: Sports Illustrated Kids: Ball | Includes webography. | Includes bibliographical references and index. | Audience: Ages 8-11 years | Audience: Grades 4-6 | Summary: "How do the best basketball players go from playing pick-up games on a neighborhood court to scoring big-time contracts in the NBA and WNBA? With hard work and determination! Discover the paths players take to turn their street ball and high school hoop dreams into college and professional careers" -- Provided by publisher.
Identifiers: LCCN 2021015988 (print) | LCCN 2021015989 (ebook) | ISBN 9781663906519 (Hardcover) | ISBN 9781663920652 (Paperback) | ISBN 9781663906489 (PDF) | ISBN 9781663906502 (Kindle Edition) Subjects: LCSH: Basketball--Vocational guidance--Juvenile literature. | Basketball--Training. | Basketball--Scouting. | Basketball players--Recruiting--Juvenile literature. | National Basketball Association. | Women's National Basketball Association. Classification: LCC GV885.1 .D646 2021 (print) | LCC GV885.1 (ebook) | DDC 796.323/64023--dc23
LC record available at https://lccn.loc.gov/2021015988
LC ebook record available at https://lccn.loc.gov/2021015989.

Image Credits
Associated Press: John Locher, 16, 19, Steve Reed, 11, Ted S. Warren, 25; Getty Images: FatCamera, 5, Jared C. Tilton, 28, Joe Murphy, 10, Xinhua News Agency, 8; Newscom: Hector Gabino/TNS, 20, John Rivera/Icon Sportswire, 24, Raddad Jebarah/ZUMAPRESS, 18, Sipa Asia/Sipa USA, 27, Wolfgang Fehrmann/ZUMA Press, 22; Shutterstock: Africa Studio, (chalk), design element, Chamnong Inthasaro, (court), design element, ChromaCo, (girl), design element, Dan Thornberg, (basketball texture), design element, EFKS, Cover;, oneinchpunch, Cover, 1, 2, SvgOcean, (word), design element, teka12, (player), design element; Sports Illustrated: Bill Frakes, 7, Erick W. Rasco, 6, 12, Manny Millan, 15, Robert Beck, 17, SI Cover, 9, Simon Bruty, 13

TABLE OF CONTENTS

Words in **bold** are in the glossary.

TAKING THE SHOT

The clock ticks down. The crowd roars. You're the star player on your high school basketball team. The game is on the line. You dribble and spin past your defender. You rise up to take the shot.

Cameras flash. College **scouts** watch from the stands. You know that this shot is just one step on your basketball journey. You have dreamed of a pro career from the time you first picked up a ball. You have spent your life playing street ball. You have gone to basketball camps. You earned your place on this team. And now, you want to show that you are ready for the next step.

You loft a shot. The ball sails through the air. Swish! It's good! You did it! But you still have a long way to go to get your dream.

A player launches a shot over his defender.

CHAPTER 1

LEARNING AND BUILDING

LeBron James. Michael Jordan. Sue Bird. It is a thing of beauty to watch the stars of the National Basketball Association (NBA) and Women's National Basketball Association (WNBA). But even the world's best ballers did not start out dropping dimes and draining threes. They had to learn the game. Players had to build on their natural talent. They spent hours on the court. They mastered their spin moves and sick crossovers.

DID YOU KNOW?

Only about 3 in 10,000 male high school players make the big time. That is a tiny 0.03 percent!

LeBron James (right) drives to the lane in a 2018 Eastern Conference Finals game against the Boston Celtics.

Tina Charles (#31) battles for position in the 2010 Women's NCAA Tournament.

TINA CHARLES: FROM THE STREETS TO THE PROS

Tina Charles played on the streets of New York City. But Charles wasn't that good at first. She didn't get chosen for pickup games.

That did not stop her. Charles kept at it. She got better. And better. Soon, she was ruling those pickup games. She was a star at the University of Connecticut. She later became a WNBA MVP. "If I'm going to be out there, I might as well be the best," she said. "And I think I'm close to that."

James Harden (right) leads drills in a camp for young basketball players.

THE BASICS

Young players work to get better. Basketball camps teach them the **fundamentals**. The kids play in local leagues and groups like the **Amateur** Athletic Union (AAU). These groups give players a taste of teamwork.

High school is where many players get a real chance to shine. High school basketball is big all around the U.S. This is where the world's best young players show their stuff for college and pro scouts.

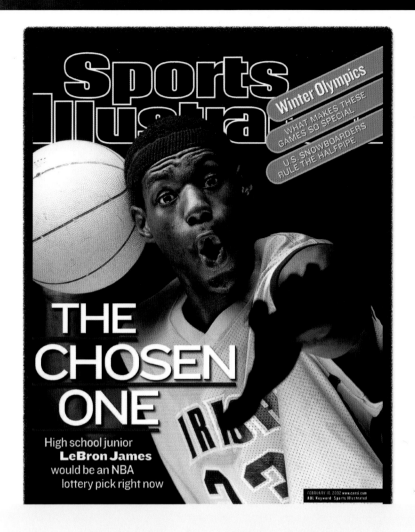

Sports
Illustrated

Winter Olympics
WHAT MAKES THESE
GAMES SO SPECIAL

U.S. SNOWBOARDERS
RULE THE HALFPIPE

THE
CHOSEN
ONE

High school junior
LeBron James
would be an NBA
lottery pick right now

FEBRUARY 18, 2002 www.cnnsi.com
AOL Keyword: Sports Illustrated

LeBRON JAMES: HIGH SCHOOL LEGEND

By the time he was 16, LeBron James was becoming a star. His size and skill made him a wizard on the court. James was on the cover of *Sports Illustrated* when he was 17 years old.

James went straight from high school to the NBA. At age 18, he was the top pick in the 2003 NBA **Draft**. He went on to become one of the greatest players of all time.

CHAPTER 2

COLLEGE BOUND

Most players go to college before the pros. There are some exceptions. But college is a must for many players. College coaches recruit the top high school players. Most give players scholarships. This is money for school and expenses. Players get this in exchange for playing on the team. Scholarships give players a chance to get an education. They can also show off their skills against the nation's best amateur players.

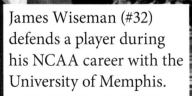

James Wiseman (#32) defends a player during his NCAA career with the University of Memphis.

BALLING OVERSEAS

LaMelo Ball took a unique path to the NBA. He left high school in his junior year to play in a pro league overseas. Ball chose to skip college. He starred on a pro team in Australia.

It was an unusual path. But it worked. The Charlotte Hornets selected him as the third overall pick in the 2020 NBA Draft. He was 19 years old.

LaMelo Ball shows off his new jersey after the Charlotte Hornets drafted him in 2020.

THE COLLEGE GAME

Each college player has four years of **eligibility**. Some leave for the pros after just one year. They are often called one-and-done players. Others stay the whole time. They grow and build their skills in games and **tournaments**. If they are lucky, they get to play in the NCAA Tournament. It is a big-time competition. It is a chance to shine on the big stage.

Two players battle for a rebound at the 2018 NCAA Tournament.

DID YOU KNOW?

There are over 350 Division I basketball programs. Each team has about 13 players. That means there are more than 4,500 men and 4,500 women playing the top level of college hoops!

Buddy Hield (right) tries to make a move against his defender in the 2015 NCAA Tournament.

BUDDY HIELD: GOING THE DISTANCE

Decades ago, most of the top players stayed in college for four years. But now, it is less common. Most top players leave after just a year or two.

Buddy Hield could have left the University of Oklahoma early. He would have been a high pick in the NBA Draft. But he stayed all four years. He was named the 2016 College Player of the Year. The New Orleans Pelicans picked him as the sixth pick overall in the 2016 NBA Draft.

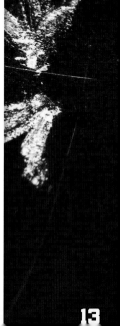

CHAPTER 3

PREPARING FOR THE PROS

Once a player is old enough, he or she can enter the draft. It is a big deal to decide when to go pro. Players have to weigh a lot of factors. How high will they go in the draft? Is there a chance they will not be drafted at all? Could they improve their draft standings with one more year of college? And how important is finishing college to them?

Pro contracts can offer huge amounts of money. Players who stay in college have to wait for that payout. They could get hurt playing in college. That could ruin their chances of playing pro ball. There is no right answer for when to declare for the draft. Each player faces a different situation.

The Minnesota Timberwolves selected Kevin Garnett (left) fifth overall in the 1995 NBA Draft. Garnett skipped college to go straight to the pros.

GOING PRO

Everything changes when a player decides to go pro. Their amateur careers are over. Now players can spend more of their time working out and training, in hopes of making a pro team.

The draft **combine** is a great chance for players to stand out. The combine is a giant tryout that takes place each spring. Players are measured. They do interviews. They perform drill after drill. Pro scouts track their speed. They watch the players shoot. They break down each player's skills. Scouts look at their passing ability and basketball IQ.

A player runs drills at the WNBA combine.

Russell Westbrook throws down a dunk in a 2011 game.

Deni Avdija of Israel speaks to reporters after being selected in the 2020 NBA Draft.

THE DRAFT

All the hard work leads to the big day—the draft. The WNBA drafts in April. The NBA usually drafts in June. The teams gather to pick players. They choose players round after round. The draft is a dream come true for some players. They wear the hats of their new teams. They talk to reporters. They meet their new coaches. It is a sad day for others. Those who are not picked face new choices. Is their dream over? Or do they need to find another way?

ERICA WHEELER: FROM UNDRAFTED TO WNBA ALL-STAR

The 2013 WNBA Draft did not go the way Erica Wheeler had hoped. No one chose the star guard from Rutgers. But she did not give up. She played overseas. A former player for the Atlanta Dream saw Wheeler play. Then she got a tryout with the Dream. She made the team. But she was cut after just one season.

In 2016, Wheeler signed with the Indiana Fever. She proved she belonged. She became an All-Star in 2019. She was named the All-Star Game MVP that year.

Erica Wheeler celebrates after being named the MVP of the 2019 WNBA All-Star Game.

MAKING THE TEAM

Getting drafted is a big deal. But there is no promise of success. Most NBA and WNBA **rookies** have to work hard just to make a team's **roster**. They learn their teams' plays in minicamps. NBA hopefuls play in the Summer League. The league is loaded with many players battling for a roster spot. It is a chance for players to show their skills. They hope to prove that they belong on a team.

The last step is training camp. It is one final cram session before the start of the season. Rookies who make the cut have finally reached their dream. It's game time!

Chris Bosh (second from the left) and the Miami Heat prepare for the season at training camp in 2015.

CHAPTER 4

BEYOND THE BIG LEAGUES

Most young players dream of knocking down clutch shots in the NBA or WNBA. But not everyone can make it to the big show. So what happens when a player does not make a team? Is it game over?

No! The NBA and WNBA are the top leagues. But they are not the only ones. Players who do not make the cut can still play pro ball. And if they are good enough, they might have a chance at the top leagues down the road.

Many women play professionally overseas. This game features European teams TSV Wasserburg and Rutronik Stars Keltern.

THE G LEAGUE

The most direct path to the NBA is the G League. It used to be called the D League. This is the NBA's minor league. G League players do not earn huge **salaries**. They do not play in front of thousands of fans. Their games are not on national TV. But the G League is the first place an NBA team looks when they need to fill a roster spot.

Jarrell Brantley (right) of the Salt Lake City Stars posts up against his defender in this 2019 G League game.

Alfonzo McKinnie (center) throws down a dunk during a 2018 pre-season game against the Sacramento Kings.

ALFONZO McKINNIE: G LEAGUE SUCCESS STORY

Alfonzo McKinnie wasn't on the NBA's radar when he finished his college career at Wisconsin-Green Bay in 2015. So McKinnie played overseas. In 2016, he tried out for the Chicago Bulls' G League team. He earned a spot. McKinnie did not waste his chance.

McKinnie went on to play with the Golden State Warriors. He was part of the Warriors team that went to the NBA Finals. In 2019, McKinnie signed with the Cleveland Cavaliers. He was then traded to the Los Angeles Lakers in 2020.

PLAYING OVERSEAS

North America is not the only basketball hotbed in the world. Europe, China, and Australia have great pro leagues. Ricky Rubio, Yao Ming, and many other players starred in these leagues. Then they went to the NBA. Stephon Marbury became a star in China after his NBA career.

Many WNBA stars play overseas too. Maya Moore is famous for winning titles with the Minnesota Lynx. But she also won with teams in Spain, China, and Russia.

DID YOU KNOW?

WNBA players can earn anywhere from a base salary of $130,000 to about $500,000. But they can make millions playing overseas.

Stephon Marbury (right) directs the offense in this 2017 Chinese league game.

PATHS TO GLORY

There are many ways to become a pro basketball player. Many players go the traditional route. They move from high school to college to the NBA or WNBA. But there are other ways to go. From street ballers to **international** stars, every player takes his or her own path. They use talent and hard work to chase their dreams.

Slovenian-born player Luka Dončić (#77) has found a successful career with the Dallas Mavericks.

BASKETBALL PLAYERS BY LEVEL

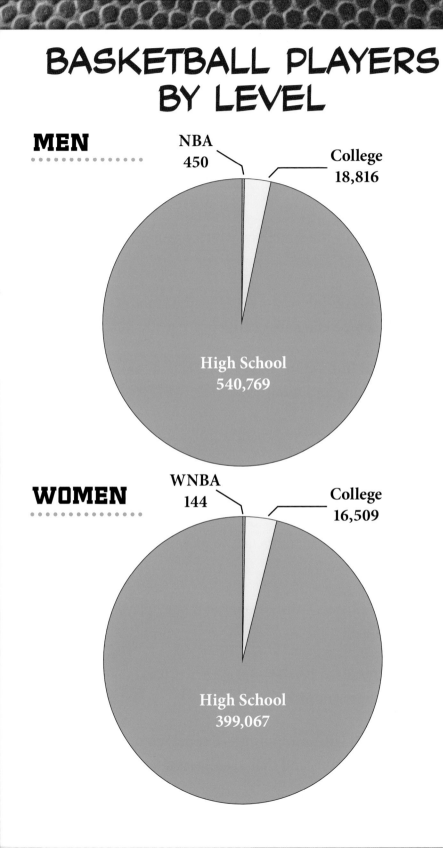

MEN

NBA
450

College
18,816

High School
540,769

WOMEN

WNBA
144

College
16,509

High School
399,067

GLOSSARY

amateur (AM-uh-chur)—a player who is not paid to participate in a sport

combine (KOM-byn)—an event where athletes complete tests to show their athletic abilities

draft (DRAFT)—the system by which pro sports teams select new players

eligibility (EL-uh-juh-bihl-uh-TEE)—the amount of time a player can compete in college athletics, usually four years

fundamental (fuhn-duh-MEN-tuhl)—a basic skill of a game, such as dribbling and shooting

international (in-tur-NASH-uh-nuhl)—involving more than one nation

rookie (RUK-ee)—a first-year player

roster (ROSS-tur)—all of the active players who make up a team

salary (SAL-uh-ree)—the amount of money players earn for playing a season

scout (SKOWT)—a person who evaluates basketball talent for college programs or pro teams

tournament (TUR-nuh-muhnt)—a sports competition that involves many teams and that usually lasts for several days

READ MORE

Doeden, Matt. *The Great Ones.* North Mankato, MN: Capstone, 2022.

Mattern, Joanne. *What It Takes to Be a Pro Basketball Player.* Mankato, MN: 12 Story Library, 2020.

Velasco, Catherine Ann. *Behind the Scenes of Pro Basketball.* North Mankato, MN: Capstone, 2019.

INTERNET SITES

NBA
nba.com/

SIKids Basketball
sikids.com/basketball

WNBA
wnba.com/

INDEX